Circle Time

A practical book of Circle Time lesson plans

This booklet was originally compiled by the Making Belfast Work – Discipline in Schools – Team and Holy Cross Boys' Primary School. The school had been involved in the Discipline Project since December 1989 and continues to develop its positive behavioural policy and practice.

Included in the booklet are the lesson plans produced by Holy Cross Boys' for pupils at Key Stages 1 and 2. These plans could also be used at Key Stages 3 and 4 – in some instances ideas may need to be adapted.

Consultant and Originator of the Quality Circle Time Model

Jenny Mosley

Illustrations by

Juliet Doyle

Published by Positive Press Ltd
28a Gloucester Road
Trowbridge
Wiltshire
BA14 0AA
England

New edition © 2001 Positive Press Ltd
Reprinted © 2004 & 2010 Positive Press Ltd
Originally published 1990 in photocopied format
with red card covers and tape binding

ISBN   978-0-953012-27-5

Printed by Heron Press
White Hays North, West Wilts Trading Estate, Westbury, Wiltshire BA13 4JT
Tel: (01373) 825602 Fax: (01373) 825603 Email: info@heron-press.co.uk

Contents

This booklet aims to:

1. Help schools implement a whole school positive behaviour approach.

2. Introduce Quality Circle Time and show how it can contribute to the enhancement of self-esteem in children and adults and create a positive school ethos.

3. Provide clear, accessible lesson plans for teachers who want to develop the approach in their classroom.

Comments from official reports

The Jenny Mosley Quality Circle Time Model has been rigorously tested over many years and endorsed by hundreds of OFSTED reports from all over the country, specifically highlighting the beneficial effects of the model. Reports often refer to particular aspects of the model such as 'Circle Time', the 'Golden Rules' or the 'Lunchtime Policy'.

Most often they note the effect of the whole school policy on the ethos of the school and pupils' moral, spiritual, social and emotional development.

'The good relationships within the school and the successful Circle Time have raised pupils' self-esteem and they know and understand what is expected of them.'

(OFSTED Report, Broadstone First School, para 26, 1995)

'The weekly Circle Time for each class enables pupils of all ages, at their own level, to reflect on aspects of their lives, to discuss moral and social issues and to express with confidence their understanding of right and wrong and their sense of justice. Pupils learn to listen to others, to be tolerant of other viewpoints and to respect fellow pupils.'

(OFSTED Report, Canberra Primary School, para 100, 1992)

In their guidance notes on Social Inclusion: Pupil Support, the DfEE (now DfES) included the following statement:

'Supporting behaviour management:

... The Whole School Quality Circle Time Model ... can help improve and maintain high standards of behaviour and discipline.'

(Circular no. 10/99, page 7, para. 2.1, 1999)

The aims of a whole school positive behaviour approach are:

1. To promote teaching and learning.
2. To enhance the pupils' self-esteem, and encourage self-respect and respect for others.
3. To encourage pupils to develop their independence through becoming responsible for their own behaviour, and achieving self discipline and self-control.
4. To develop interpersonal skills which facilitate co-operation with others, problem-solving and rational conflict-resolution skills.

These aims contribute to:

1. Educational achievement
2. Emotional security
3. Personal growth
4. Moral development
5. Socialisation

It is important to remember that *all* members of staff need to be involved in policy making.

A policy is an agreed course of action, and in the case of behaviour policy spells out what conditions are required for teaching and learning to take place, how teachers might set these conditions up and what resources, skills and management techniques they need to know.

In a consistent and well-maintained positive behavioural policy all adults need to:

1. Positively promote good behaviour.
2. Be clear with the children what they can and cannot do (rules).
3. Constantly recognise those children who keep the rules (i.e. a balanced combination of rewards and punishment).
4. Plan to deal with unwanted behaviour in a manner that is likely to reduce the behaviour recurring (i.e. don't reward children for bad behaviour).
5. Let everyone know there are rules and make it in everyone's interest to keep them – children, teachers, ancillary workers, parents, governors.

The Elton Report

Although written over a decade ago, the Elton Report, *Discipline in Schools* (HMSO 1989) is an extremely important document. It made recommendations about actions 'aimed at securing the orderly atmosphere necessary in order for effective teaching and learning to take place'.

Elton's findings support the view that teachers are beaten down, not 'beaten up' (as the press would have us believe) by constantly dealing with 'relatively trivial but persistent misbehaviour'.

The report's findings identify 15 indicators of a 'good school'.

Good schools:

1. have a positive atmosphere based on a sense of community and shared values.
2. have a headteacher and senior management who take the lead in plans for good behaviour.
3. Have a Code of Conduct and values represented in formal/informal curricula which reinforce one another.
4. Have a high degree of consensus about the standards of behaviour among *staff*, *pupils* and *parents*.
5. Have clear guidance for staff, parents and pupils about standards and how to uphold them.
6. Recognise good behaviour and consistently praise it.
7. Deal with bad behaviour.
8. Have ways of ensuring that the punishment fits the deed and is fairly and consistently applied.
9. Have a sense of collective responsibility led by a headteacher who promotes this in staff and pupils.
10. Work as a team to develop whole school approaches to promote good behaviour.
11. Examine carefully content and delivery of curriculum, and motivation of less able pupils in particular.
12. Promote mutual respect, self-discipline and social responsibility.
13. View pastoral care as a vital ingredient in the total educational experience of the child and use support agencies effectively.
14. Take pride in school buildings.
15. Have effective ways of communicating with parents.

The Circle Approach as a practical response to the Elton Report

Circle Time meetings take place weekly and last between 20 and 50 minutes according to the pupils' age and their ability to concentrate. The circle approach involves the whole class group (30+) and the teacher sitting in a circle.

The teacher's task is to present a programme of circle activities that will most effectively challenge and motivate the class group to share in the aim of promoting more positive relationships. You can choose activities from a wide range of co-operative games, rounds, drama strategies, talking and listening exercises, puppet and mask activities, according to the ages and abilities and needs of that particular class group.

Through these activities and their subsequent discussion children are encouraged to develop emotional literacy, think more about their own behaviour and its effect on others, and share in the responsibility for creating a better learning and caring atmosphere. For example, being called names upsets children. During circle sessions, if they are kept emotionally 'safe', some children may take the opportunity to talk about the misery this name-calling causes them. One child, whose surname was Dyer, was constantly called 'diarrhoea', another child, Adrian, was continually taunted with the name 'Aids'.

When motivated through the Quality Circle Time approach to think about solutions to the problems that their behaviour causes themselves and their peers, children can devise many inventive systems to help foster their aims. One class decided that they talked far too much and consequently were not working as they would like. They arrived at the solution of making 'do not disturb' signs which they could put on their tables to signify the times they wanted to concentrate and remain undisturbed.

One class and 'their' troubled child worked jointly on an action plan with certain behavioural targets that had to be reached by that child; if he achieved these then they agreed to let him play football with them. 'Help each other be good' became one of their class rules.

Children's own written comments, however, certainly reflect their appreciation of the benefits. They say that circle time helps with –

finking

I think it is to here everybodys veiws on somthing.

TO LeArm and TO Think
Things over
and TO Think Thing, out

Their answers reflect an acknowledgement that they are beginning to think about their behaviour and their interpersonal relationships and to feel more confident about their own role in being able to change these situations. These pupils were being encouraged towards a sense of feeling part of a group.

Teachers' evaluations reflect that they now understand the point of regularly using the circle approach with their classes. Included below are a range of comments in response to the question: 'Having taken part in this circle programme, what value do you think this Circle Time approach may have for the participants?'

↓

Builds up self-confidence self-esteem.

Creates a group feeling.

encourages a responsible attitude to the groups behaviour

Makes individuals aware of others feelings + needs.

If you don't boost self-esteem it will lead to:

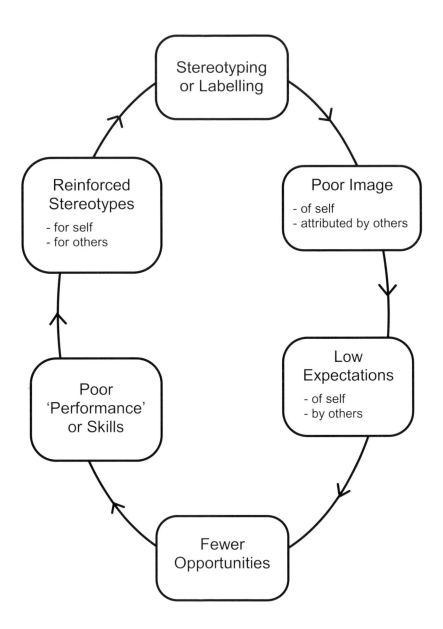

NEGATIVE AND CUMULATIVE CYCLE

Why we believe Quality Circle Time is beneficial

Rationale

Quality Circle Time affords the opportunity for the teacher and class to communicate with each other about issues which promote self-esteem and positive behaviour.

Quality Circle Time aims to develop:

1. The value and self-confidence of each child

2. Specific behaviours which show caring and respect towards each other (e.g. 'do be kind when others make mistakes').

3. The establishment, in an enjoyable and constructive way, of classroom routines that are necessary for quality teaching and learning.

4. A climate of good relationships between teacher and children and child to child.

5. A way of meeting children's needs with regard to improving their behaviour, rather than saying 'What they deserve is …'

6. Talking and listening skills in a way that helps such skills transfer across the curriculum.

7. A sense of responsibility for one's own behaviour and actions.

8. An environment that is non-threatening where teachers and pupils can express themselves and listen to each other.

The following material has been produced by some of the teachers of Holy Cross Boys' Primary School, Belfast.

Setting up Quality Circle Time – essential prerequisites

- Sitting in a circle – eye contact
- Establishing ground rules, e.g. hands up
- Taking turns
- Allowing children to 'pass'
- Valuing *all* contributions – no put-downs
- Always praising – very positive
- Low teacher profile
- Always ending session on a positive note
- Making it fun – light-hearted

Preparation

1. Have class sitting in a circle (preferably on chairs and in their own classroom environment).

2. Teacher is a participating member of the circle and, although directing activities, abides by the 'rules' of the circle.

3. Ensure Circle Time is not interrupted as it should be 'quality' time with the group. A good idea is to use the 'Do Not Disturb' sign outside the classroom door – a sample is included in this booklet.

4. Have your lesson plan carefully thought out in advance and have ready for use a 'conch' or talking object for rounds (held by the person speaking), musical instruments, music cards, story ideas etc.

5. Try to have Quality Circle Time as a regular part of your classroom activity, i.e. at a regular and set time so that children see it as an important part of their school week.

LESSONS FOR KEY STAGE 1 (Year group 1)

Lesson 1

Introduction

Class and teacher agree ground rules. Examples:

Hands up	Look at person who is speaking
Take turns to speak	Listen well
No put-downs	

Activity 1

General participation games, e.g. passing on smile – teacher looks at next child to pass on a smile.

1. Pass on rain, i.e. hands raised up and down, fingers wiggling – touch next child to pass it on.

2. Pass on thunder i.e. stamping on floor – touch to pass it on.

Listening	– point to ears	)	
Thinking	– point to head	)	Get class to follow teacher's
Looking	– point to eyes	)	actions
Well done	– fold arms	)	

Activity 2

Musical Round:
Musical instrument – try to pass around silently – e.g. tambourine, bells.

Activity 3

'Bag of Sweets' Game:
Teacher says 'Imagine you have a wonderful bag of sweets on your knees. Think of what you have, e.g. is it Smarties, jelly babies etc. Now you're going to share it with the person next to you.' Then everyone stands up and offers sweets to others – don't forget to thank people. Choose certain children.

Activity 4

 'Talking Ted'
('Conch strategy' using small teddy or any special item as talking object):
Each child has the opportunity to speak or pass. Simply stand and say name or 'pass' and pass object to next boy/girl. 'My name is ... and I like ... sweets.'

Final Activity – Evaluation

Each child has the opportunity to say what they liked best about today's circle time; (use 'hands up' or conch strategy).

Lesson 2

Introduction – Rule reminder / Establish rules

Activity 1

Simple number or word games – general participation:
Children are standing. They say 1, 2, 1, 2, 1, 2 around the circle. Any child who gets it wrong sits down. Continue until all children are seated or you think the children are losing interest.

Activity 2

Experiencing silence – sit quietly, be very still. Now pass an object round without a sound, e.g. keys, bells, tambourine. See how quietly the children can do this.

Activity 3

'Fruit Basket' Game:
Children are named oranges or apples. Oranges change seats when teacher calls 'Oranges', apples change seats when he/she calls 'Apples'.
(Fruit basket – all change – add later, if class are competent).
Modification for younger children – 'oranges' are given an orange-coloured item such as building block, 'apples' are given a green one, as constant reminder of what they are (or coloured dots on their jumpers).

Activity 4

'Talking Ted' Round:
Pass Ted round circle; teacher begins by saying:
'I like ...' e.g. TV programme, food. 'I don't like ...'
Each child takes a turn – remember to allow a child to say 'Pass'.

Final Activity

Pass the Squeeze:
Children and teacher hold hands around the circle. The teacher gently squeezes the hand of the child on his/her left, who then squeezes the hand of the child on his/her left and so on until the 'squeeze' has passed round the circle and back to the teacher.

Lesson 3

Introduction – Rule reminder

Activity 1

Games of 'Follow the Leader':
Teacher does action while class copy, e.g. teacher claps, child follows. Clap hands, touch knees etc.
Progress to child being leader when class feel competent.

Activity 2

a. Listening – Children sit with eyes closed, teacher has instrument. Teacher uses musical instrument, then stops. Children put up hands when sounds disappears.
b. Progress rhyme such as – (1) 'Head, shoulders, knees and toes', then 'Head, shoulders, knees and …' (2) 'There was a farmer had a dog, and Bingo was his name oh, B-I-N-G-O, B-I-N-G-O, B-I-N-G-O and Bingo was his name oh' – leave out letters in order, e.g. B-I-N …, replacing them with silence.

Activity 3

'Talking Ted' Round:
Round begins – 'I feel happy when …' (child can pass).
Children who pass should be given another opportunity to speak at conclusion but should only speak when they are holding Ted / the conch.

Activity 4

Activity Game:
e.g. Children standing inside circle. One clap – walk. Two claps – stop. Three claps – walk on spot.
Teacher is leader initially; eventually child could do clapping.

Final Activity – Evaluation

Any child can put their hand up to say what they liked best about today's circle time – or what they didn't like.

Lesson 4

Introduction – Rule reminder

Activity 1

a.   Game of 'Simon Says' – explain do 'this', do 'that' only when Simon Says.

b.   Listening – point to ears)
       Thinking – point to head)   Children copy teacher
       Looking – point to eyes)   while repeating words
       Well done   – fold arms   )

Activity 2

Looking and Listening Game:
Collection of three instruments, e.g. tambourine, bells, cymbals.
Chosen boys/girls (by eye contact, touch or holding conch) to pick up instruments quietly and pass three around simultaneously (begin with one, then two, then three instruments).

Activity 3

'Talking Ted' Round:
Introduction by teacher using a short story about the experience of an imaginary child. 'Daniel has started a new school. It is his first day in the playground at lunchtime. He watches all the other children playing happily together. None of the children have talked to Daniel or invited him to join in their games. He feels very lonely and sad. '
Begin a round with 'I feel sad when ...'. Those who pass may be allowed a turn at the end of the round.

Activity 4

Game of 'Statues':
Children walk round to beat of instrument, e.g. drum. Freeze when beat stops.

Final Activity

Statues slowly melt onto the ground.

Lesson 5

Introduction – Rule reminder

Activity 1

Round Game:
Teacher begins by saying 'I am sitting beside ...' (giving next child's name).
Next child speaks so that the phrase is moving round the circle from the teacher.
Then/or 'My friend is ...' (giving next child's name).

Activity 2

Musical Game:
Moving to simple beat, e.g. drum or tambourine.
Heavy steps, fast steps, light steps, slow steps – echoing appropriate beat.
Instrument stops, then children stop.

Activity 3

'Talking Ted' Round:
Teacher tells a story about two friends. Amit and Josh are good friends. They spend all their spare time together. They like to cycle, play on their skateboards or challenge each other at computer games. Amit and Josh always try to be considerate and helpful to one another and to share both good and bad things. 'That's what friends are for,' they say.
Round begins –'I can make my friend happy by ...' (children may say 'pass').

Activity 4

Imagination Game – 'The Magic Wand':
Teacher has a magic wand, waves it and says 'You are all elephants/ mice/ rabbits' etc. Children pretend by doing actions inside the circle. Pass wand to child to try.

Final Activity

All hold hands around the circle. On the count of three, all raise hands in air and say together, 'It's good to have friends!'

Lesson 6

Introduction – Establish / Revise Rules etc.

Listen well
Hands up
Take turns to speak

Look at person who is speaking
Smile

Activity 1

Expression Game:
Children cover faces with hands. Teacher says:
1 Smile
2 Frown (or look angry)
3 Laugh (silently i.e. mime)
4 Cry (silently i.e. mime)
Children remove hands to reveal appropriate expression.
Pass a smile around the circle.

Activity 2

Musical Instruments Game:
Two different instruments, e.g. xylophone, glockenspiel.
Two children in middle to play as they like. Then first child to sit down, second child moves to first instrument and next child goes to free instrument. Teacher guides by calling out each change until everyone has had a turn.

Activity 3

Cue Game:
Everyone to change seats, or put hands on head, on cue.
Teacher to talk to class about any subject. Tell class that on hearing cue word they must perform an action, e.g. 'I am going to talk about the weather, every time you hear the word RAIN, put your hands on your head'.

Activity 4

'Talking Ted' Round:
Children to speak in turn while holding Ted – 'My teacher is ...' (name of teacher); 'My room is room ...'; 'I go to ... School'
Start with one statement, progress over weeks to three statements.

Final Activity

All hold hands around the circle. On the count of three, all raise hands in air and say together, 'We all like Circle Time!'

Lesson 7

Introduction – Establish rules etc

   Listen well
   Hands up
   Take turns to speak
   Look at person who is speaking

Activity 1

Follow the Leader:
Simple game – general participation.
Children hum the same note. When teacher raises hands they get louder,
when teacher lowers hands they get softer. When teacher moves hands apart
they stop. Vary speed of hand movements.

Activity 2

Making Sounds (round or hands-up game):
Try to make noise without using anything other than chair or floor, e.g.
1. Make a loud noise with hands – go round circle – praise any novel ideas.
2. Make a soft sound with feet.

Activity 3

Cue-card Game:
Teacher has two cards, one red, one black. Children to stand in circle.
When shown red card, march around noisily.
When shown black card, tiptoe round.
Children must watch carefully as cards are changed without warning.
Children who miss change of card sit down.

Activity 4

'Talking Ted' Round:
Children to speak in turn while holding Ted (or conch etc). Can say 'Pass'.
'I like to be noisy/quiet (make choice) because ...'

Final Activity – Evaluation

As Lesson 3.

Lesson 8

Introduction – Establish rules etc

Listen well
Hands up – Take turns to speak
Look at person who is speaking
No put-downs
No laughing at mistakes

Activity 1

Changing Seats Game:
Simple game – general participation.
All stand. Teacher calls child's name, e.g. 'Mary', and then changes places with that child and sits down. Mary then calls name, changes places and sits down. This continues until all children are seated.

Activity 2

Listening Game:
Teacher has selection of musical instruments in centre of the circle. Children close eyes and listen. Teacher makes a sound with one instrument. Children put up hand if they know which one made the sound.
A child who is correct then chooses and plays next instrument.

Activity 3

Sound Game:
Teacher makes animal sound and touches next child to pass it round the circle. When the teacher says 'Stop', next child chooses new animal sound and so on until he/she says stop and process goes on.
(Teacher could give/receive ideas beforehand).

Activity 4

'Talking Ted' Round:
Teacher talks about 'personality traits' in the context of how we think of different animals, then begins a round, 'If I were an animal I would be a ... because ...'. Children can say 'Pass'.

Final Activity – Evaluation

'What I liked best about today's Circle Time was ...'

Lesson 9

Introduction – Rule reminder

    Listen well
    Hands up
    Take turns to speak
    Look at person who is speaking

Activity 1

Action Game:
Simple game of passing around the circle – general participation.
Teacher starts with two actions (or one action if children find this difficult),
e.g.   1. Clap hands, stamp feet
        2. Touch nose, nod head
Pass it on.

Activity 2

Musical Repetition Game:
Two drums in middle. Teacher beats drum up to four times, then calls name of child who copies. Then child calls another and he/she beats, to be imitated by new child, continuing round class.
Variation – someone beats drum, everyone responds by either clapping or stamping same number of times.

Activity 3

Imagination Game:
Teacher says 'You have a new toy.' Stand up. 'You are going to let a friend play with it.' Find a friend, swap toys, tell them what the toy is. Don't forget to say thanks. Teacher says 'Back to your seat' and then children may tell what they borrowed.

Activity 4

'Talking Ted' Round:
Children think of a toy they would like to give to the child on their left. If someone elects to pass, another child can volunteer to take his/her turn as well as their own.

Final Activity – Evaluation

As Lesson 3.

Lesson 10

Introduction – Rule reminder

> Listen well
> Hands up
> Take turns to speak
> Look at person who is speaking

Activity 1

Mime:
Simple game – general participation. Teacher leads.
Miming activities involved in going to school each morning –
1. Wake up – rub eyes, stretch, yawn
2. Wash face and hands
3. Get dressed
4. Eat breakfast
5. Off to school

All change seats. Repeat.

Activity 2

Musical Movement Game:
Children standing. Two instruments used. Children are light elves (glockenspiel) or heavy giants (drum). Must listen and respond; stop when teacher stops playing. Let child have a turn with the instruments to make the others become elves or giants.

Activity 3

'Caring Ways' Game:
Teacher tells a pretend story that the boy or girl beside you has fallen in the playground. What would you do/say? In turn, starting with teacher as role model giving evidence of verbal and physical sympathy (e.g. patting child 'there, there'), turn to next child and show sympathy. Pass round circle.

Activity 4

'Taking Ted' Round:
Teacher begins by saying
'When someone helps me I feel …'

Final Activity – Evaluation

As Lesson 3.

LESSONS FOR KEY STAGE 1 (Year group 2)

Lesson 1

Introduction – Establishing rules

> Listen well – (arms folded, looking, listening) – praise.
> Hands up to ask a question – praise only those who remember to raise their hands.
> Look at the person who is speaking.

Activity 1

'Passing-on' Game (see page 13):
Passing on a smile – change to rain. First child will use his or her fingers to represent falling rain – then pass it on to next and process continues; (teacher may go over quietly and demonstrate to any child having difficulty).

Activity 2

Listening Game:
Teacher takes a chime bar and gives an instruction with a sound – hands up or touch knees – children obey only when they hear sound of chime bar and not the instruction on its own.
Change movement and repeat.

Activity 3

'Talking Ted' Round (conch strategy – see page 13):
Teacher begins round, 'I feel happy when …'
Explain the right to say 'Pass' but offer the conch/Ted back at end of each round.

Activity 4

'Bag of Sweets' Game (see page 13):
Offer a sweet to your friends – go around the class.

Final Activity

Teacher says, 'Close your eyes – imagine you are eating your favourite sweet. Think of its taste and texture in your mouth. Think how much you are enjoying it.'

Lesson 2

Introduction – Rule reminder

Activity 1

Action Game:
Do actions – thinking (hands on temples), listening (ears), looking (eyes), well done (arms folded). Teacher leads by calling for actions – children respond.

Activity 2

Listening Game:
Like 'Simon Says'. Teacher uses chime bar – gives instructions but class obey only when they hear three sounds.
(The words 'Simon Says' are not spoken. These words are represented by the three chime bar sounds.)

Activity 3

'Talking Ted' or Conch Round:
First brainstorm all the things that make the children feel sad.
Begin round – 'I feel sad when …'
Teacher or volunteer may begin round.

Activity 4

'Fruit Basket' Game:
Children are either oranges or lemons (teacher goes round and touches all oranges on shoulder, then lemons). When calls out 'Oranges' they change seats, when 'Lemons', they change. On the words 'Fruit Basket' everyone changes seats.

Final Activity – Evaluation

Round: 'The part I liked best today was …'

Lesson 3

Introduction – Rule reminder

Activity 1

Follow the Leader:
First child makes any action – passes it on. Later the teacher explains that the action can be changed by another child but must be copied or changed again. (You will find only the most confident children will change the action at first, while quieter ones just copy).

Activity 2

Listening Game:
Pick a child to take chime bar – give instruction for class to follow when they hear the sound, i.e. class will obey the instruction only if it is accompanied by the sound of the chime bar, e.g. walking inside circle or tapping knees while sitting on chair or floor.

Activity 3

'Talking Ted' or Conch Round:
'My favourite animal is …'
Remember rule that allows child to say 'Pass'.

Activity 4

Imagination Game – 'The Magic Wand' (see page 17):
Child takes magic wand (can be a ruler) and changes a few children into animal of his/her choice – they imitate animal and then one takes wand to repeat the process.

Final Activity

Round Game:
Listen – concentrate on sounds outside for two minutes. Tell one sound heard – choose a child to begin round with 'I heard …'

Lesson 4

Introduction – Rule reminder

Activity 1

Action Game:
Teacher names children 1 to 4 around the circle and allocates an action to each number. When he/she calls e.g. 4 – every fourth child around the circle stands up and performs action (e.g.hop on the spot) etc. Teacher then calls another number. Can alternate what each number does by giving simple instructions.

Activity 2

Listening Game:
Have selection of instruments in the middle of the circle – teacher winks at a child who creeps out quietly – takes an instrument and returns to his/her place in silence, then winks to another child etc. If the child makes a noise with the instrument he or she has to leave it back in the circle.

Activity 3

'Talking Ted' or Conch Round:
Begin 'I wish I was …' (e.g. a favourite place, a famous person).

Activity 4

'Follow the Leader' Game (using sound):
Marching around circle – teacher uses a drum –
One beat equals **walk**
Two beats equals **stop**
Three beats equals **walking on the spot**
Teacher may allow a child to use the drum while he/she joins in

Final Activity

Close eyes – relax – think of something happy.
Do a round and tell us your happy thought.
(Use conch or other talking object and remember to allow child to say 'Pass'.
Offer those who passed a turn at the end.)

Lesson 5

Introduction – Rule reminder

Activity 1

Passing-on Word Game:
Someone starts 'car' going round circle by saying 'zoom' and looking to child on right. Word and action passed round quickly till someone (can be teacher at first) says 'eek' to change direction, then the zoom sound goes round the other way.

Activity 2

Musical (Listening) Game:
Instruments in the centre. Teacher has notation cards colour-coded red for loud, black for soft.
Child gets a wink – picks up an instrument quietly and plays the number of notes on the card which is held by the teacher. Remember to encourage the child to play loud or soft according to colour code. (If you do not think your class are familiar with musical notes then just use numbers or dots).

Activity 3

'Talking Ted' or Conch Round:
'If I were a magician I would …' (think of something good to 'magic' for the other children to enjoy.) Remember rule about passing.

Activity 4

'Follow the Sound':
Use a drum to make a choice of sounds – soft/loud or quick/slow etc. Children march according to sound, i.e. tiptoeing quickly or plodding slowly according to the instruction from the drum. Teacher explains the movement that should follow the sound.

Final Activity

'Talking Ted' or Conch Round:
Begin 'What I like about Circle Time is …'

Lesson 6

Introduction – Establish / revise rules

Listen well
Hands up – wait your turn
Look at person who is speaking
No laughing – no put-downs.

Activity 1

'Simon Says' (see page 16).

Activity 2

Sound Game:
Choose a child to take a chime bar or tambourine etc. Children must respond to *two* sounds this time, not one, i.e. one sound – no response, two sounds – walk, stamp, clap etc. (Teacher says which movement children should make and when to change the movement).

Activity 3

'Talking Ted' or Conch Round:
Teacher talks about dreams.
Begin round, 'A dream I had was …'

Activity 4

'The Magic Wand':
Child takes magic wand – changes *whole* circle into an animal, e.g. pig. All get into centre and imitate that animal – then change.

Final Activity

Listening and Telling Round:
Sit down, close eyes – listen to sounds *outside* classroom – do a round to tell us what you heard. Teacher may begin 'I heard a bird' then pass conch object to next child etc.
Remember to offer children who pass another turn at the end of the round.

Lesson 7

Introduction – Rule reminder

Activity 1

Passing-on Sounds:
Pass on a sound, e.g. animal noise / weather noise. Any child can change sound but circle must keep passing it on.

Activity 2

Sound Game:
Repeat Lesson 6, Activity 2 from this section: i.e. chime bar – two sounds – respond to an instruction *only* when accompanied by *two* sounds from chime bar.

Activity 3

'Talking Ted' or Conch Round:
Begin 'The best day in my life was when …'

Activity 4

Fruit Basket Game:
Repeat Lesson 2, Activity 4 from this section: i.e. children are named as oranges and lemons. Call 'Oranges' – oranges change seats, 'Lemons' – lemons change seats, 'Fruit Basket' – all change seats.

Final Activity

'Talking Ted' or Conch Round:
Teacher says 'Eyes closed, imagine you are on a beach – sun shining – tell us what you see/hear'. Begin 'I could see ...' or 'I could hear ...'

Lesson 8

Introduction – Re-establish Circle Time rules

Activity 1

Zoom Game:
Repeat Lesson 5, Activity 1 in this section. 'Zoom' passed on very quickly – any child can change it to 'mooz' – whereby it changes direction and goes back.

Activity 2

Listening Game:
Repeat Lesson 4, Activity 2 in this section: i.e. have a selection of instruments in the middle of the circle. Teacher winks at a child who creeps out quietly and takes an instrument and returns to his/her place in silence. Having returned, the child winks to another child who then carries out a similar process (this has already lowered teacher profile).

Activity 3

'Talking Ted' or Conch Round:
Teacher talks about magic and making wishes etc. 'What would you do if you were a magician for a day?' Each child chooses one thing to say.
Begin 'I would …'

Activity 4

Treasure Hunt / Obstacle Game:
Teacher chooses a child as 'Guardian' to sit on chair in middle of circle, wearing a blindfold. Teacher puts keys (treasure) under chair and places obstacles in circle. Child must climb obstacles and retrieve treasure in *silence* – 'Guardian' must catch him/her (by pointing to where the sound is coming from). If the Guardian succeeds then he/she can choose the next Guardian of the Treasure.

Final Activity

Play a piece of music while children sit in silence, eyes closed. Teacher says 'Think of what you see in your mind's eye.'
Children put up hands to tell what they saw.

Lesson 9

Introduction – Rule reminder

Activity 1

Expression Game (see page 18):
Children cover face with hands – teacher describes something which could have happened to them (happy/sad) – take away hands and show expression – then change.

Activity 2

Repeat Lesson 8, Activity 2 in this section.

Activity 3

'Talking Ted' or Conch Round:
Teacher talks about when the children were babies, toddlers etc.
Begin 'When I was small I always used to …'

Activity 4

'The Magic Wand':
Child points to another with the wand – that child goes into the centre and mimes action of an animal – rest must guess what he/she is (*hands up*). Child who guesses correctly can have the wand.

Final Activity

'Sharing Sweets' Imagination Game:
Imagine a bag of sweets – describe what it is. Pick a child – *not* a friend – someone you don't normally talk to – and offer them a sweet. Remember to say thank you.
Continue inside circle until teacher says 'Stop'.

Lesson 10

Introduction – Rule reminder

Activity 1

Finish a Story (Conch Round):
Teacher begins story –'The Broken Cup'. Sean asks mum can he invite his friends for a garden party – yes, you can, but don't use any of my good cups – he agrees – takes old cups out of the garage – mother gives lemonade – pretend tea – friends come – he pours – each have a cup – except himself so he looks through kitchen window at new cups. What did he do?
Begin 'Sean …'

Activity 2

Musical (Listening) Game:
See Lesson 5, Activity 2 in this section. Instruments are in the centre of the circle. Teacher has notation cards, colour-coded red for loud, green for soft. The teacher winks at one child who picks up an instrument quietly and plays the number of notes on the card. Remember again to encourage the playing of loud and soft according to colour-code. The child goes back to his place and he winks at another child who carries out the same process.

Activity 3

Round:
Teacher asks class if they sometimes worry. Discuss.
Begin 'Sometimes I worry about …'

Activity 4

Ball Game – 'Follow the Teacher':
Give a bouncing ball to each person in circle. Teacher begins by bouncing the ball – nods at a child who imitates teacher at same pace – watch teacher – child stops when the teacher stops. This can be done with whole group.

Final Activity

Music Round:
Play music – listen – is it happy/sad? What do you feel? (Teacher should choose a piece of music carefully for this activity).
Begin round 'I felt sad/happy …' Pass conch.

LESSONS FOR KEY STAGE 2

Lesson 1

Introduction – Establish rules

> Hands up
> Listen well
> Look at speaker
> Only speak when conch / talking object is with you
> No laughing at others
> No put-downs

Activity 1

Treasure Hunt (see page 30):
Put chair in middle of circle with 'treasure' (something that rattles e.g. keys) underneath. Put a couple of obstacles to climb over, e.g. bin is a bear pit, book is a rock. 'Guardian' sits on chair wearing a blindfold.
Total silence in group. Child to 'steal' treasure without Guardian hearing.
If successful he/she picks that child to go next as Guardian. Repeat.

Activity 2

'Simple Simon' Chime Bar' Game:
Similar to Simple Simon except children obey rules only if chime bar is hit, i.e. say 'sit down' – no response, say ' sit down' and hit chime bar – children sit down.

Activity 3

Conch Round:
Discussion of rules. 'Conch' is chosen (something valuable like an ornament), person speaks only when holding conch – ability to say 'Pass' is allowed.

Final Activity

Breathing exercises to end on quiet, settled note, i.e. six deep breaths inhaling and expelling air. Finish lesson.

Lesson 2

Introduction – Rule reminder

Activity 1

'Magic Wink' Game:
Class sitting quietly in circle, arms folded. Teacher picks one child to be in middle. Another child from circle is magician – he/she winks at child who falls on floor asleep – child in middle must guess who magician is.

Activity 2

Sound Game:
Discrimination of sounds. Three children pick different instruments and the rest of the group close eyes. Instruments are hit and children must guess what instrument is being played; (important that they raise hands, no shouting out). Teacher can wink at the child he/she wants to play instrument.

Activity 3

Conch Round:
Discussion of 'My worst habit' – again conch passed around, pupils in circle decide who will speak next by *hands up*. Establish rule of no laughing and no put-downs and praise those who are honest.

Final Activity

Lie on floor – listen to music – children think about what feelings it evokes. Finish.

Lesson 3

Introduction – Rule reminder

Activity 1

'Hunter and Hunted' Game:
Children stand around circle. Teacher chooses two children, one wears a blindfold and is hunter, other is quarry, both inside the circle (absolute silence). Hunter tries to catch prey by sound of feet moving – if he/she goes to edge of circle, other children gently direct him/her back into middle.
Change children.

Activity 2

Movement to Sound:
Children stand in middle of circle and move on spot to beat of bouncing ball, drum or similar. Important they find their own spot, no bumping into one another.

Activity 3

Conch Round:
Teacher talks about what makes us upset or annoyed. Begin round, 'One thing that really annoys me is …'. Again conch is passed around – children allowed to say 'Pass' – no laughing, no put-downs. Offer those who pass a chance to speak at the end of the round.

Final Activity

Children stand in snowman pose and imagine the sun shining on them. They slowly melt until they are 'puddles' on the floor. A quiet activity designed to wind children down.

Lesson 4

Introduction – Rule reminder

Activity 1

'Follow the Teacher' Game:
Simon Says – teacher gives instructions, children follow only when teacher prefixes with 'Simon Says'.

Activity 2

Musical Instrument Game:
Children in circle are given different instruments and follow beat of the leader. (The leader does not have to be the teacher).

Activity 3

Conch Round:
Teacher talks about things we say/do to hurt others – people we would like to say sorry to; (be careful here, children tend to force the issue, i.e. make up reasons to apologise). This is a good activity after some major problem in class – fights etc. Begin with volunteer who says 'I would like to say sorry to …' Pass conch to any other volunteer; n.b. get child to *look at* the person and *say their name* when they are saying sorry.

Final Activity

Listen to sounds outside room for one minute with eyes closed.

Lesson 5

Introduction – Rule reminder

Activity 1

'Fruit Basket' Game:
Children sit on chairs, one child stands in the middle. Children are labelled oranges or lemons. Child in middle calls out either oranges or lemons and those called change places while child in middle tries to get a seat. When successful, child from middle takes on identity of child he/she is replacing. No pushing or shoving or fighting over seats.

Activity 2

Musical (Listening) Game (see page 27):
Children given cards with blobs, dots, notes, numbers etc, red for loud or black for soft. Child gets a wink, picks up an instrument and plays number of notes on card which they have. Remember to encourage children to play soft or loud according to card.

Activity 3

Conch Round:
Teacher talks about what should happen when rules are broken. Begin round asking what sanctions should school have? Get children's suggestions. Use conch, hands up, no laughing, shouting or criticising. Praise good suggestions. Allow child to say 'Pass'.

Final Activity

Children form a line based on different characteristics, e.g. biggest to smallest. Do this quietly and without rushing. Teacher may supervise closely. Teacher talks to children about ways in which we are all the same. Children put hands up to offer suggestions.

Lesson 6

Introduction – Rule reminder

Activity 1

'Lighthouse and Rocks' Game:
Choose a lighthouse – give him/her a tambourine or drum with which he/she makes an infrequent sound. Choose a ship – the captain wears a blindfold – rest of group spread around floor as rocks – captain has to steer around rocks to lighthouse – rocks clap when he gets near.

Activity 2

Spot the pupil:
Teacher of group relates a lot of information about someone in group – children guess who is being discussed. Remember *Hands Up*.

Activity 3

Things We Like (Conch Round):
Discussion on what makes us feel good, e.g. 'I like it when …'
Conch passed around – no laughing at each other.

Final Activity

Rhythms and Beats:
Question and answering session. Leader beats out a rhythm (clapping) which children echo. Children can also volunteer to lead clapping.

Lesson 7

Introduction – Rule reminder

Activity 1

Mantle of the Expert – imagination game:
Leader is chosen from group – he/she has been invited to a special school for witches and wizards because he/she has invented a new spell; a special one that no one else thought of. He/she has to describe it. Two or three children take turns to tell story – volunteers only.

Activity 2

Musical Game:
Place four instruments in middle, e.g. chime bars. Leader has a chime bar – four pupils in middle numbered 1-4. Leader plays his/her chime bar (any rhythm) – child number 4 copies this then goes to his/her seat. Number 3 moves to 4, 2 to 3, 1 to 2, new child is number 1. They all repeat tune. Continue until all have had a go.

Activity 3

Conch Round:
Discussion on their favourite parts of school, – subjects, interests etc. Begin 'In school I like …'

Final Activity

Children sit quietly with eyes closed. Teacher plays chime bar or cassette tape of gentle music, and only when sound dies away do children open eyes. Repeat.

Lesson 8

Introduction – Rule reminder

Activity 1

Points of Contact Game:
Children pass 'body parts' around the circle, i.e. elbow to elbow, knee to knee.
End by passing a smile.

Activity 2

Movement to Sound:
Children all stand in middle, teacher blows whistle – one short blow means
walk – one long blow means run on the spot – two short blows mean hop –
two long blows mean walk backwards – no touching, bumping etc.

Activity 3

Feelings:
Teacher makes a facial expression e.g. sad, happy, worried. Children guess
or teacher identifies feelings that children will discuss, such as worry, envy;
e.g. 'I worry when …', 'I am sad when …', 'I hate it when …'
Again no laughing or criticising.

Final Activity

Play some fairy music on glockenspiel or a cassette tape of suitable music.
Children tiptoe quietly inside circle. When music stops children must *freeze*.

Lesson 9

Introduction – Rule reminder

Activity 1

Buzz Game:
Children number around in circle – 1 - 2 - 3 - buzz, 5 - 6 - 7 - buzz (i.e. mustn't say multiples of 4). Whoever misses buzz is out. Very good for learning tables.

Activity 2

Musical Statues:
Tambourine is jingled – children run on spot – if it's hit they stop. (Progress to running around in circle without touching.)

Activity 3

Finish the Story:
Teacher tells story of marbles. Two children, Paul and John, started with ten marbles each – Paul lost all his to John – he was lonely, he thought about going home – John now had twenty marbles. What happened next? Pass conch, teacher comments on positive endings. Begin 'I think John/Paul ...' Allow to say 'Pass'.

Final Activity

Stand up, close eyes tight, you are a block of ice. Teacher improvises story about being washed up on a beach and melting – lie absolutely still until teacher claps hands – then stand up quietly.

Lesson 10

Introduction – Rule reminder

Activity 1

Charades:
Teacher picks child to mime activities of particular jobs – teacher goes first miming postman – child who guesses right mimes next.
(Good idea to have a list of jobs to choose from.)

Activity 2

Making Sounds:
Use the Wind Poem on the next page.

Activity 3

Conch Round:
The world would be a better place if everyone … – children discuss their opinions.
Begin 'I think the world would be better if …' No put-downs. Allow children who pass a chance to go at the end.

Final Activity

Follow the Teacher:
Teacher makes some simple movements – children follow – tapping knee and touching head etc.

The Wind

Poem with vocal and other sounds or instruments

The wind has lots of noises	*(spoken words only)*
it sniffs	*(vocal sounds on each line, appropriate to the words)*
it puffs	
it whines,	
it rumbles like an ocean	*(drums or drumming hands)*
through junipers and pines.	
It whispers in the windows	*(vocal sounds on each line, appropriate to the words)*
it howls	
it sings,	
it hums,	
it tells you very plainly	*(spoken words only)*
every time it comes.	

This gives an example of how sounds can be used with the poem.
Decide on your own instruments/sounds.

TRAINING AND RESOURCES

Training for your staff

The Jenny Mosley Consultancies can provide well-trained consultants, experienced in all aspects of the Whole School Quality Circle Time Model, who will visit your school to run courses and workshops for teachers and support staff. Try our key introductory course for primary and secondary schools on the **Whole School Quality Circle Time Model**:

- On a Closure (INSET) day, all staff, teachers, lunchtime supervisors, ancillary and administration staff are invited to participate in a day that focuses on all aspects of the model, including team-building, developing positive ethos and valuing individuals.

- On a Working In School day, the school does not close and the Quality Circle Time approach is demonstrated with whole groups of pupils observed by a range of staff. In addition, Circle Time meetings can be held for lunchtime supervisors and an action plan for the school is drawn up with key members of staff.

- The Top Value Option (discounted price) is to book both the above plus a follow-up day for evaluation and advice.

Other courses for schools

The following are examples of courses offered by our team of highly qualified and experienced consultants, available in similar format to the above:

> Happier Lunchtimes
> Assessing the effectiveness of your self-esteem, anti-bullying and positive behaviour policies
> Developing peer mediation
> Developing PSHE, Citizenship and emotional literacy policies through Quality Circle Time
> Re-energising your circle time policies with *Quality* ideas
> Children beyond – what more can we do?
> Involving everyone in Quality Circle Time

Accredited, specialist trainers only!

Our research and experience reveal that the Whole School Quality Circle Time Model can become diluted or vulnerable when people who have never attended one of our in-depth courses offer training based on our model. Jenny Mosley holds week long in-depth courses nationally and then awards accompanying certificates.

For details of all the above, contact the Project Manager by any of the means listed on page 48. A list of accredited trainers is available.

Books and other resources

Turn Your School Round by Jenny Mosley
Comprehensive management manual for the whole school community to develop positive relationships through circle time. (LDA)

Quality Circle Time by Jenny Mosley
Essential guide to enhancing self-esteem and self-discipline, for teachers wishing to put the Whole School Circle Time model into their classrooms, with hundreds of ideas and lesson plans. (LDA)

More Quality Circle Time by Jenny Mosley
Develops the application of the model in a sequel to the above. Includes ten-minute circle times for nursery children to practice specific skills. (LDA)

Here We Go Round by Jenny Mosley & Helen Sonnet
Delightfully illustrated book of Quality Circle Time activity plans for the Early Years in response to the QCA guidance document, with sessions for each of the six areas of learning. (Positive Press)

Photocopiable Materials for use with the Jenny Mosley Circle Time Model by Jenny Mosley
Charts, target sheets, achievement ladders, awards, congratulations cards, invitations and much more. (Positive Press)

Circle Time ed. Jenny Mosley
User-friendly low-budget, high-value booklet, with excellent lesson plans for reception, KS1 and KS2. (Positive Press)

The Circle Book by Jenny Mosley
Inspiring collection of responses to Quality Circle Time, with feedback from teachers and children and great suggestions for games and activities. (Positive Press)

Working Towards a Whole School Policy on Self-Esteem and Positive Behaviour by Jenny Mosley
How to write and operate an effective policy involving teachers, children, parents, MDSAs – everyone! With background information and ideas based on schools' experience using the Quality Circle Time model. (Positive Press)

Bridging the Circle: Transition through Quality Circle Time by Anne Cowling and Penny Vine
Thoughtful and effective Circle Time lesson plans for years 6 and 7 supporting the often intimidating transition from primary to secondary school. With photocopiable resources.

All Round Success by Jenny Mosley
Simply set-out practical ideas and games to help children with their social skills. (WEST)

Coming Round Again by Jenny Mosley
Sequel to All Round Success, outlining how to pull together a range of fun activities into a themed approach. (WEST)

Guidelines for Primary Midday Supervisors by Jenny Mosley
A friendly, practical self-help booklet to be given directly to lunchtime supervisors as part of the policy to boost their skills and self-esteem. (WEST)

Assemblies to Teach Golden Rules by Margaret Goldthorpe and Lucy Nutt
Dynamic and fun assemblies for developing the moral values behind Golden Rules, based on positive reward for good behaviour rather than punishment for negative actions. (LDA)

Poems for Circle Time & Literacy Hour by Margaret Goldthorpe
Poems of simplicity and fun, to help children look at serious issues in a relaxed way within our five-step model. (LDA)

Effective IEPs through Circle Time by Margaret Goldthorpe
Practical solutions to writing Individual Education Plans for children with emotional and behavioural difficulties, using Quality Circle Time. (LDA)

Positive Playtimes – exciting ideas for peaceful playtimes

Stepping Stones to Success – a planned journey through the foundation stage

Ring of Confidence – personal safety for the foundation stage

101 Games for Self-Esteem

101 Games for Social Skills

We also have books on Quality Circle Time for Secondary Schools.

Training DVD: Quality Circle Time in Action
An excellent in-depth resource for staff training, showing Jenny demonstrating her model with KS1 and KS2 pupils. Includes booklet with her five steps to Quality Circle Time. (LDA)

Jenny Mosley's Self-Esteem Builders Set
Contains motivational stickers for congratulating children on moral values and circle time skills; two colourful themed class target sheets with reusable stickers to mark positive behaviour towards a particular target; reward certificates for achievements such as deciding to improve; responsibility badges for boosting children's self-esteem through special tasks such as being special child of the week; and a golden rules poster set for classroom and playground. **Items also available separately**. (LDA)

Jenny Mosley's Kitbag of Power
Contains 2 soft puppets, free Puppet Scripts booklet, gold fabric, rainstick, Rainstick booklet, blindfold, wand, QCT DVD, talking egg, gold box, bean bag and booklet of kitbag activities.

Contact details for Jenny Mosley Consultancies / Positive Press Ltd:

28a Gloucester Road, Trowbridge
Wiltshire, BA14 0AA, England
For Training Enquiries
Telephone: 01225 767157
Fax: 01225 755631
E-mail: circletime@jennymosley.co.uk

For Products and Resources
Telephone: 01225 719204
Fax: 01225 712187
E-mail: positivepress@jennymosley.co.uk

Website: www.circle-time.co.uk